to my new
forever friend—
  Dot ~
Thank you for finding me
Thank you for encouraging me
and thank you for helping me up
the paths of the many mountains ahead.

  It's all about
  the Climb—
    Twila

Climbing the Mountains

Climbing the Mountains

Twila Zehr Patterson

CROSSBOOKS
PUBLISHING

CrossBooks™
A Division of LifeWay
1663 Liberty Drive
Bloomington, IN 47403
www.crossbooks.com
Phone: 1-866-879-0502

Scripture taken from the King James Version of the Bible.

First published by CrossBooks 07/07/2011

ISBN: 978-1-4627-0543-6 (sc)
ISBN: 978-1-4627-0544-3 (hc)

Library of Congress Control Number: 2011933674

Printed in the United States of America

This book is printed on acid-free paper.

This book is dedicated to my family. I would only have hills to climb, not mountains, if it weren't for each of you! (Then life might get a little boring!)

Troy, Tanner, Tiana, and Tessa, I will be with you every step of the way, no matter what.

I can do all things through Christ which strengtheneth me.
—Philippians 4:13

Foreword

When we began our lives as a married couple, my wife and I were on the top of the world. Nothing could stop us now. What problems in life could be so bad? As the title of Twila's book, *Climbing the Mountains*, suggests, we ran into problems. How do you deal with mental illness? How do you help two bipolar kids through life? How could we help our kids have a normal life? Why us, God? Those are some of the questions that come up daily. As you read through my wife's book, you will see some of the struggles we have gone through and see how God has helped us through. You will see God's hand on our lives to give us the strength and wisdom we needed to help our kids. My prayer is that God will use us as a family to touch the lives of others who are going through struggles with mental illness. I am very proud of my wife and can't think of a better person to go through the highs and lows with. She is the rock of our family.

I love you, honey bunches of oats!

—Troy

As Twila's mom, I have been with her as she has climbed the mountains in her life. I'm amazed at all she has accomplished during the difficult struggles she has had to face. There are times she is doubled over in pain with tears flowing. Then on some days, we act crazy and laugh together!

So, day by day, we keep on following Jesus, *taking* one step at a time *because* through it all, *someday it* will be worth it all.

—Marge Zehr Bowman

Our family theme song is "The Climb." There's always going to be another mountain, and we're always going to want to make it move. How are we going to handle the climb?

Contents

Chapter 1

Growing Up

I grew up in a normal family. Well, at least I think we were normal! We lived in a small town called Berne, Indiana. Some people call it little Switzerland. You don't have to use turn signals in Berne. Everybody knows everybody, and they all know what you are doing or where you are going. While I lived in Berne, there was only one stoplight, and that was by the elementary school. We lived in a white house with red bricks. My dad was a printer, my mom a secretary, and I have an older brother named Brock. We walked to school each day and walked home each afternoon. My best friend was Michele. Oh, the fun times we had together.

The basement was our toy room. Every month we made decorations to hang from the ceiling—January snowflakes, February hearts, March shamrocks. You get the idea. My brother hated these things and would often jump and hit them off the ceiling. We mainly made these decorations to tick him off. It worked! One wall of our basement was a chalkboard, and we went through many boxes of chalk. We played with Barbie, dolls, played teacher, rode our matching orange ten-speed bikes around town, and went to the pool and park. It was a great, normal childhood—exactly the kind of childhood I wanted for my own kids someday.

As we grew older, we attended the same church and were very involved in the youth program. I was known for playing "Do Lord" on the kazoo and singing duets with Jodi, another childhood friend. Our youth group would compete in various contests throughout the year and would go to national competition in New York during the summer. This is where I would later spend a year of life going to college and traveling with a singing group. Jodi and I came in second at nationals one year singing "More Than Wonderful." I would love to be able to sing with her just one more time, but that will have to wait until I get to heaven. Jodi was killed in a car accident in 1989. That was really the first death I ever had to face except for my grandparents.

I had no idea at the time that a year later my life would be forever changed. I do remember during the next year I had a recurring dream. I was getting married. I never saw the groom, but my dad was not walking me down the aisle; it was my brother. I couldn't figure out why Dad wasn't doing his job of giving me away. I had this dream about three times, and then it all came together on March 22, 1990. Now I am getting ahead of myself, so let's go back to my childhood.

Brock and I had paper routes. That is a lot of work—rolling the newspapers, riding your bike with a big bag full of newspapers, throwing the newspapers, and not hitting doors/windows. As I look back now, those are some of my best memories. We were good kids. The worst thing we ever did was break a lamp in the basement while playing baseball. We would often make a mess in the kitchen while throwing cereal up in the air and trying to catch it with our mouths. Once we turned our stereos on high and put the same song on. The walls rattled. We were just normal kids. We were both on the church Bible quiz teams.

School was easy for Brock, and he always got good grades. I only did well in the subjects I liked. He later married Becky Liechty, his high school sweetheart. Now they have two boys, Brad and Ben. I babysat my nephews for years and will always cherish those special times.

My dad was a quiet man, but when he spoke, you listened. My mom, on the other hand, is very outgoing. I started off like my dad, but I am turning into my mom. I am not commenting if that is good or bad! My dad was a writer. He wrote great articles for the local newspaper. Later he went into the printing business, and then in 1987, he opened his own print shop. This was a dream come true for him, and he named the shop ZIP (Zehr Instant Printing). Catchy, isn't it!

My mom was the church secretary and very involved in the children's program at church. It was called Whirlybirds. We wore little beanies with plastic helicopters on them. We had to earn buttons to be sewn on our hats. The fuller the hat, the cooler you were. It was the '70s. What can I say? My husband and I can still sing the Whirlybird theme.

Yep, my husband and I grew up together in Berne. Troy and I were great friends. Later when I went away to college, I was hoping to find my future spouse, a guy just like Troy Patterson. Well, there were no Troys at college, but I did meet another best friend, Jenny. Words cannot explain her! Everybody thought I was the most stuck-up snob, but Jenny realized I was just really shy. Twenty-plus years later, we are still very close. She even sends her daughter to our house in the summer to be my mini-mommy helper for a few days. We have a lot in common, and Jenny will always be a special part of my life. Berne, Indiana, was a great place to grow up, and I am very thankful for my Christian heritage. See, I really did have a normal childhood. My sorrow is that my kids will never know what normal is.

The song "Jesus Loves the Little Children" comes to mind as I write this chapter. He loves all the children in the world. Will society love my children just like God does?

Chapter 2

Some through the Fire

As I mentioned earlier, my dad was the owner of his own print shop, ZIP. He was also very intelligent. He could carry on conversations with anyone. He knew a little bit about a lot of things. His passions were family, music, reading/writing, and cutting coupons. He was thrifty. In the late '80s, Dairy Queen had a good deal going on: burger, fries, drink, and a sundae for $2.95. This was only on Thursday nights, and he always told my mom that was his night to cook. He stocked up on grocery deals too.

The steps to our basement were right beside the chalkboard wall. We would have to draw around his many cans stacked on the stairs. I liked to organize them by color, size, and kind. I had issues even when I was young! My dad had many books. He was always reading, but he was good at it. He could have five started at the same time, switch off reading, and still remember what they were all about. My dad loved music. Records were always being played in our home. My daddy sang bass! He was in a men's quartet called the Missionaries. As I am writing this, I can hear him singing. My favorite song they sang was the "Old Country Church." He had a special solo part and would go real low and sing, "I have been redeemed." My dad was a wonderful Christian man. He was well thought of in the community, was a hard worker, and was so kind.

After I graduated from Word of Life Bible Institute in Schroon Lake, New York, I came back to Berne and lived with my parents. I worked at the local grocery store, with my mom for a few months and then got hired as a bookkeeper at the downtown Berne bank. I loved my job. Sometimes during my afternoon break I would walk to Dad's shop and visit.

His life was way too short. At the age of forty-eight, on March 22, 1990, the dad I loved so much never returned home. I can still remember hearing him say that morning, "Remember, Dairy Queen tonight." He left for the shop, my mom left for work at the store, and I left for the bank, and six hours later our life as we always knew it was gone. At 1:30 p.m., there was a big boom outside. One of the bank employees yelled my name, and I went running outside. That is when I saw the fire. Our print shop was only half a block away, and it was consumed with flames. I met my dad at the front door, where he was crawling out on his hands and knees. Somebody threw their coat over him to snuff out the flames.

I screamed, "Dad, are you okay?"

He said, "Yep, I'll be okay."

Those were the last words any of us were to hear from him. I quickly went across the street and called my mom. I said, "Dad's okay." She thought he was really okay; I meant he was alive. We were not allowed to ride with him in the ambulance. There were just too many people who had to work on him, and the burns were very raw. We called my brother who worked in Fort Wayne, where the burn center was located, and told him what happened. He met the ambulance at the hospital.

A friend followed the ambulance and took my mom and me to the hospital. The first time we saw Dad was in the emergency room. There was blood leaking through the bed. His back had gotten the brunt of the explosion. His face and hands were burnt, there were tubes down his throat, and he couldn't talk, but his eyes said everything. He was scared, and he was so sorry to put us through this. We all told him we loved him and that the explosion was not his fault. He understood this, and then they sedated him. While in the waiting room watching TV, we heard what had happened to ZIP through a live news report. A gas line had been cut by a company. They had time to evacuate and chose not to. When the furnace ignited, the shop exploded and blew my dad to the front door.

There are times when I don't even believe this really happened. We were just a normal family—not rich, not poor, just normal. My dad did nothing to deserve this punishment. I was mad at God. Our lives took on a whole new meaning. My brother actually wrote a manuscript about this tragedy, but it never got published. For the next six months, our lives were in complete shock. My dad couldn't live and he couldn't die. During the first few weeks in the burn center, he had a stroke during one of the many skin graft surgeries. He was not Dad from that moment on.

My mom and I drove the hour trip one way each night when I got off work. We celebrated all our birthdays, Brad's first birthday, and Father's Day while he lay in a hospital bed. His kidneys were not functioning, and he was put on dialysis. We had a choice to make: let him live or let him go to heaven. We all chose heaven. A week later, we were in his hospital room and watched him take his last breath.

The next day was my mom and dad's twenty-eighth anniversary. To celebrate, Brock and Becky had bought front-row tickets for a very special concert with Bill Gaither and friends. This had been planned since January, and we were all looking forward to attending. My mom insisted that we all go to the concert because that is what Dad would have wanted. He was going to watch the concert from heaven instead. Someone had told the musicians about Dad's death, and they dedicated the song "Because He Lives" to our family. We cried, we sang along, and we got to personally meet the singers. It was a big night, and I know my dad was rejoicing in heaven with no more pain.

The next day was his viewing, and his funeral was on September 10. My mom wanted a celebration of his life, so she invited all the men in the community to come sing in a men's chorus. Forty men took off work that Monday afternoon to honor my dad, Mike Zehr. Reflections of his life were read, music was sung, and many tears were shed. Another chapter of life was about to begin, and it was going to be a very hard mountain to climb.

Do you know how cruel people can be? Berne is a very small town, and sometimes that is a good thing and sometimes not so good. Everybody wanted to know everything that was going on during the lawsuit we had to file. My dad's hospital bill was over $1,000,000. Our attorneys advised us to keep our mouths shut, which we did. Still to this day, there are only a handful of people who know what happened. Many people were upset with us because we were not sharing every detail of our lives.

When you go through a tragedy, you certainly find out who your true friends are. There was one person who sent a note every week for a year. There were many people who really cared. Then there were others who said, "It has been three months, snap out of it." I had a very hard time working in the public eye at the bank. I eventually quit because I couldn't handle people anymore. Some even had the nerve to say, "Only people with sin in their lives had bad things happen to them." I knew this was not true, but that comment has scared me ever since. This is when my depression battle began.

One of my favorite songs is "Because He Lives." I had no idea how many mountains were ahead of me, but I knew He would help me face each tomorrow. Life was worth living just because He lives.

Chapter 3

Come-to-Jesus Meetings

Eventually my mom and I moved to Fort Wayne, Indiana. That was huge for us. Many Berne people wondered why we would move away from a small community. Basically, I needed to start over, and my mom helped me do this. She bought a great house on a little lake. We were ten minutes from the mall and only fifteen minutes from Brock and Becky's house. My mom and I are still very close. She told me not to write a whole chapter about her but to just splash her in the pages. You never know when she will appear. It is one of those *bam* moments, there she is!

During this time in life, we spent hours playing games, going to southern gospel concerts, shopping, and healing. Life was looking brighter. I became an exercise fanatic. I was finally able to handle stress and life. My depression was being controlled with medication. God was helping me get my life back again.

I was still looking for a Troy Patterson to complete my life but couldn't find one in the city. Then we went back to Berne one evening for a "God with Us" concert that local churches were performing. Troy was playing trombone in the orchestra. We had not seen each other for over seven years, and all of a sudden our age difference didn't mean anything. He is five years younger than me, but most people guess it is the other way around because his hair is loose and gray. Maybe my dream would come true and I would actually get the real Troy Patterson!

He soon got brave and asked me out on our first date. It was putt-putt with two of his siblings and their significant others at the time. I was a little leery about a whole family affair but soon learned the Pattersons were a very close family. One thing I do remember about that night was Troy's huge feet. They are size thirteen, and he calls them skis. His hands are huge too, and he calls them mitts! Another thing I remember was that I kept tripping over the hills on the golf course. He said I was falling for him already. I think it was God warning me there were going to be lots of hills before the mountains came.

We dated for a few months. His family made me go mudding as an initiation into the family. A city slicker does not do such things, but you do when you are in love. My family thought we were a great match. He proposed. Now I have to tell you something here. My whole life I wanted a dog but only got cats. Troy had his own toy poodle, Tasha, and she came along with him. It was a two-for-one deal, so I definitely said yes to him. I was ready to spend the rest of my life with my "bestest" friend.

We got married in Berne, after waiting almost an entire year. My mom made us go through all the seasons before we could get married. She says each season brings out different characteristics in everybody. Whatever! I wanted a Christmas wedding, but Troy said we were not going through any season twice, so I made it as Christmassy as possible in June. There were tons of white lights in plants and netting instead of trees and garland, white magnolia flowers everywhere, burgundy and gold splashes of color, and lanterns with candles. Can you tell I love decorating!

My brother walked me down the aisle, and my dad watched from heaven. The music was fabulous. My roommate from college, Robin, and Troy's buddy, Chuck, came together and sang "More Than Wonderful" in memory of Jodi, my childhood friend who had died. We had our own Sandi Patti and Larnelle Harris! We even sang a duet together at the kneeling bench, "Only God Could Love You More Than I Do." We then thanked 325 family and friends for coming to our wedding while "Silent Night" was being played on the organ. We all ate super steaks (Berne meat) and were surprised with a hay wagon ride through town. I was kind of prissy back then, so it was huge that I even sat on the hay.

That night we went to our home. Troy got hives in the middle of the night. I guess I was just too much for him! We went to the grocery store at 3:00 a.m. to buy Benadryl. Wasn't I a nice wife, going along with him? We got up a few hours later to leave for our honeymoon to Alabama. Troy locked us out of the house before everything was packed; the first hour in the car was very quiet. I was thinking, *I am not real sure I like this marriage thing.* I was so mad Troy had not loaded everything in the car before locking us out. After our come-to-Jesus meeting, I came to the conclusion there were stores along the way to buy whatever didn't get packed.

Now let me tell you about come-to-Jesus meetings. My father-in-law, Bob, invented them. He would call family meetings whenever there was a problem. He talked, we listened, and we all hugged and said we loved each other even if we didn't feel like it at the time, and then life went on. I don't like those meetings.

Anyway, on our road trip to Gulf Shores, we listened to the cassette tape of our wedding, and for entertainment I would feed Troy Skittles, and he had to guess what color he was eating. How pitiful and boring our life was. We had driven about twelve hours and Troy said, "Next exit is our reservations for tonight." I took care of the whole wedding, and he was supposed to take care of the honeymoon. He made reservations at a brand new hotel, and he got a great deal. He was so proud. We drove up to the hotel, and a sign said, "Coming soon." The hotel wasn't built yet. I felt another come-to-Jesus meeting coming on, but I was going to be in charge this time. He quickly got on the phone, and yep, there had been a mistake, but if we went one more exit, we could stay at the executive suite at a nearby hotel. We got into our fancy room and wanted to take a soak in the Jacuzzi, but there was a little sign that said, "Jets don't work." We went down to the whirlpool, and there was a sign that read, "Under construction." I should have seen all these as signs of things to come.

We decided to go eat at a nice restaurant. We waited forty-five minutes, and the rolls were hard and the meal was gross. We went to bed hungry and grouchy. In the morning, we ate at a breakfast buffet. I believe we ate a pound of bacon each. After another day of driving, we finally made it to Gulf Shores. I love the ocean! I love to go out in the deep and just let the waves knock me around. Not Troy. He is very cautious and likes to stay knee deep. Well, I talked him into going out deeper. Life was perfect, not a care in the world. We were on our honeymoon. Yep, marriage is great. Then Troy realized we were really out in the waves and the current was pulling us farther away. We were on inner tubes and way out by the booies. Troy quickly jumped off and started swimming us to shore. Good thing he was on swim team for years. When we were safe in the sand, we had our third come-to-Jesus meeting in three days. I thought, *Yep, marriage is great.*

"Only God Could Love You More Than I Do" will always be *our* song!

Chapter 4

My Little Buddy

Tanner Lee

Early in our marriage, we found out we had a 1 percent chance of ever having a baby. We were devastated. We had always wanted to be parents. We talked about this during our engagement. Before we were married, we decided we would adopt if need be. At the time, we never thought that would be an option, but God knew all along. It was hard to be around people. It seemed everyone was having a baby but us. I fell into deep depression.

Family friends let us use their condo by the ocean for a week. That was a huge turning point in our lives. We spent hours on the beach talking about our possibilities. We each made pro/con sheets. Our main concern was adopting a baby and finding out something was wrong with it. Could we handle not having a normal life? After much prayer, we made a huge decision. We were going to adopt and accept whatever life God had planned for us. Now we had to go home and tell our families.

They were all very supportive, but I knew there were red flags in their minds. What if we spent a lot of money and never get a baby? What if emotionally we couldn't handle the ups and downs of the adoption process? Believe me, we also had all those fears going through our minds, but we really felt this was God's plan for us. We hired an agency from California and waited. The wait was not long!

I remember the day we were matched. I stayed home all day waiting for the phone to ring. There were no cell phones back then. I paced, I read, I prayed, I sang, and I paced some more. Troy was driving semi at the time and knew nothing about my day. The agency had called early that morning and said there might be a match for us and to be patient and wait by the phone. Well, I am not good at being patient. I want things to happen immediately. I continued to sit with the phone in my hand and worry.

Finally at 3:30, the birthparents called to interview me. It's a good thing it was over the phone and they couldn't see the sweat pouring off of me. We talked for about thirty minutes, each of us asking questions. My concern was prenatal care, which there had not been much of. I was also concerned about family history. They wanted to know about our lives, jobs, home, and families because they actually had picked another family to raise their baby but were having doubts. The agency wanted them to talk to one more family, which was us. We felt God was in control. We all just clicked with each other.

I had a note written for Troy when he came home from work. It said, "Get on the phone, we might have a baby!" The four of us talked another thirty minutes, and then they said they would call back with their final decision. Click! Are you kidding me? When are they calling—today, tomorrow, never? Don't leave us hanging like this. Remember, I am not a patient person. I am a planner. I need to know. I don't like surprises.

I was crying, and Troy was trying to calm me down. I was a nervous wreck. Troy then prayed a sweet prayer, saying if it was God's will for us to be parents, they would call. Just then the phone rang; it only took them minutes to decide we were their answer. Praise God from whom all blessings flow! The baby boy was due in ten days, and the state they were from did not have adoption laws in our favor. We asked them to come to Indiana. They left that night for a twelve-hour drive. We called our families for guidance, support, and prayer.

Of course, then the what ifs began. What if they came and decided they didn't like us? What if this was a hoax and they just wanted money? What if something was wrong with the baby? We had to put our fears aside and trust in God—not always an easy thing to do. We met them early the next morning at a local hotel we had booked for them. The four of us quickly got to know each other. We sent them off to sleep, and we went shopping. It had only been five weeks since we hired the agency. We had nothing for a baby, so Wal-Mart here we come! We spent the day getting the nursery ready.

That night they came to our home for supper. Over the next ten days, we entertained them and waited for our son to be born. On August 4, Troy's birthday, he left to haul his semi load to Michigan. Soon after he left, our birth mom called to say she was in labor. Today was the day! Wouldn't this be the best birthday gift ever! Seriously, we needed cell phones back then. After spending several hours in the hospital, the time was getting closer for his birth. I called Troy on his emergency only truck phone, and he told me he was two hours away. He asked me to stall the delivery. I wanted to smart back and say, "No problem, Sweetie, I will get right on that." But of course I didn't say that. I am a nice wife!

In my panic, God took care of everything. He let Troy have a lead foot and not get stopped. Troy actually made it on time and walked into the room just as our baby was being born. I thought he was going to faint. Our son, Tanner Lee Patterson, was here! Our baby's birthparents said, "Congratulations, Mommy and Daddy" and had the nurse hand him to me. What an emotional time. Here was a couple willing to give us the gift of life. God was in control, and we were so thankful. They will forever hold a special place in our hearts. Our families came, and what a birthday celebration we had! How sweet to hold our newborn baby.

We had to wait twenty-four hours for the paperwork to be signed. Were they really going to say good-bye to him? Were they going to change their minds? Were we ready to be parents? Oh, the what ifs again. Our attorney met us at the hospital the next day, and everything went as planned—no regrets, no tears, just happiness on both sides. It was time to send them back to their state and for us to start a new life as a family. For years I sent monthly pictures and letters. Slowly, over time, that all changed.

Boy, were we proud parents! We were thrilled to have a baby of our own—not flesh of our flesh, not bone of our bone, yet miraculously still our own! My dream came true. I was a mommy! Troy and I were young and had no idea how much life would change with a baby in the house. For some reason, Daddy never heard the crying in the night. I think it is a man thing! The first night, Tanner only slept three hours; he was not fussy, just very awake and alert. I am thinking, *No problem, he just has his nights and days mixed up. I can change that.* The next day he only slept three more hours. Okay, six hours in a twenty-four-hour period. This was a problem. I am a girl who really needs her beauty sleep. I need eight hours a night or I get ugly. I knew from that day on life was never going to be normal ever again.

I knew something just wasn't quite right with Tanner; I just didn't want to admit it. After a few months, I had a come-to-Jesus meeting with Troy. I let him know what I thought and that we were going to have a long road ahead of us. Many meetings were called over the next five years, but Troy denied there was a problem. When Tanner was in kindergarten, Troy finally heard me. At the age of six, our son was diagnosed with bipolar disorder. The waves came crashing in around us. I do remember his birth mom calling when he turned two years old. She had recently been diagnosed as bipolar, and her doctor wanted us to know that. At the time, I Googled bipolar and thought, *That is not going to happen to our son.* I guess I was in denial too.

Bipolar disorder, where do I begin? It is a horrible mental illness that affects not only the person with the illness but the whole family as well. So, yes, this was another really low time in my life. I was mad at God for allowing an innocent little child to suffer. In the back of my mind, I kept hearing the remarks from years ago: "This is happening because you have sin in your life." I was so depressed. I just wanted a normal life for my kids, but it was never going to happen.

My days were consumed with my little buddy. Every day I coordinated our outfits and even put matching bows in our dog Tasha's hair. I know, issues! Tanner was a great little boy. He just didn't need much sleep. He could stay up all night and still keep going the next day. On Saturday mornings, I got to sleep in. Troy and Tanner watched truck videos together, ate popcorn, and drank diet caffeine free coke. At the age of one, he could carry on conversations with an adult. He was obsessed with certain subjects, trucks being one of them. He knew every name of every truck. I think Daddy had something to do with that.

He didn't like his paci (pacifier). He would spit it as far as he could and then gut laugh. He was ornery. One day he decided to surprise me with a drawing. He was in the dining room, and I was making lunch in the kitchen. He said, "Mommy, come see what I made you." I walked into the room and there was a magnificent semi-truck drawn on our cream-colored walls. Did you know that washable markers aren't washable off walls? I'm just sayin'!

One day he took all my colored post-it notes and hung them on the front window. He wanted our house to look like a church. Then there was a time when he was mad at me for not letting him have candy. He decided he was running away from home. He got out his wagon. He put his bunny, his favorite truck, and a pair of underwear inside of the wagon, and off he went down the driveway. Then he realized he couldn't cross the street, so he came back home.

He was a spitting image of Dennis the Menace when he was little. We still love that movie! Tanner likes hot weather, not cold. He does not like to be alone, he is very verbal, and he eats really strange things. He loves onions and eats them like apples. I am sure some of his teachers have not appreciated me letting him eat them for breakfast! He hates cereal. He makes mustard, ketchup, and cucumber sandwiches. He was and still is a mama's boy. Tanner also has a heart of gold.

While he was a toddler, we were trying to adopt again. We were having a really hard time finding a committed birth mom, and one day I just cried. He came and cuddled up on my lap and said, "Mommy, God will give us a baby when He is ready." That put me in my place. He was right; God was in control, not me. I was so proud of Tanner. He was actually learning what we were teaching him.

We sent Tanner to preschool and realized school was going to be a battle for him. He was really smart but not book smart. When he was in the second grade, his teacher helped us get him the help he needed. The school set up an IEP (individual education plan) for our son, and he started going to special education. We were so thankful for help, but at the same time, we were devastated. He was going to be pulled out of the normal classroom. He was not going to be normal, ever. It was hard putting him on medication in kindergarten, but this was even worse. I really felt like a failure as a mom. I struggled again, but I knew God was never going to give me more than I could handle, although I did pray that maybe He could give me a break.

It's hard to watch your kids be sad. Tanner just doesn't have many friends. I believe he has been invited to maybe four parties in thirteen years. The outlook for his life isn't real bright. He will never get a diploma, and we have no idea if he will be able to handle a job or live on his own. He is little (just hit one hundred pounds at age thirteen and a half) but mighty. He is obsessed with shoe size, weather, the NFL, and banging the door frames in our home. Seriously, I hear the bang at least fifty times a day when he is not at school. Anything out of the routine sets him off. School delays and cancellations do him in.

His dream has always been to work with his dad at the state highway department. We doubt that will happen. He is about four years behind his peers. He has also been diagnosed with ADD and Asperger's, which is a form of autism. That explains his obsessions over so many things in life. We can only tell him one thing at a time to do. You can't say, "Brush your teeth, go to the bathroom, and wash your hands." He will have no idea what to do. We list everything in steps. He loves to "work" with Uncle Brock at his vending business. For pay, Tanner gets to pick out which restaurant to eat at. He does anything for food, just like his daddy!

He is also involved in Special Olympics. What a great program to build up special needs kids. Is it hard watching our little boy struggle in life? Absolutely. I feel so helpless at times. The bipolar rages are uncontrollable. During these rages, the hitting, verbal abuse, and threats are mind boggling. Bipolar behavior is scary. There are major mood swings that are very unpredictable. This illness is not fatal, yet a part of people with bipolar disorder dies with each rejection they receive. Bipolar kids are the first to be blamed and last to be chosen.

In their minds, they have done nothing wrong; it is always someone else's fault.

Discipline is very hard, because they do not realize what they are doing is wrong. We have holes in our walls, many dishes have been broken, and we often feel very defeated as parents. Of course, some people blame us for our parenting techniques. I would love to see them handle a rage. Medication helps, but the mental illness never goes away—never. Anything out of the normal routine can trigger a rage. They also have night tremors. When this happens, it is time for another medication change. I am here to tell you, a full moon and bipolar disorder do not mix.

Bipolar people have manic times where they just don't need sleep. They are on a constant high and cannot stop talking, moving, or pacing. I am worn out by the end of the day. Summers are very tiring. It's a good thing we are involved in the Wildcat baseball program. You really can't understand the life of a bipolar person until you watch it for yourself. Anybody want to come spend the day with me? When the rages happen, I just want to give up, but I can't. God gave us this family for a reason, and I will fight for my kids forever. Tanner kisses and hugs me more than the girls do, but I don't mind. He is my little buddy.

One of my favorite singers, Ernie Haase, wrote the song "God Give This Child a Good Heart." My prayer is that all our kids will have hearts that love Jesus, even during the really rough climbs.

Chapter 5

My Little Angel

Tiana Michaela

We wanted just one more baby. Tanner was two at the time, and we thought it was time to start the adoption process again. We filled out the mountains of paperwork, had a home study done, and waited. We knew the wait would be longer than it was for Tanner—five weeks was just unheard of—but we didn't think it would take two years. We had many phone interviews with birth moms—well, I did—and they would pick us. We would get our hopes up, only to have them be ripped away. I think we had about seven girls change their minds on us. Of course, I took this personally, and the depression came back with a vengeance. What was I doing wrong? What was I saying wrong? Why doesn't God hear my prayers?

Well, He was listening; God just wasn't ready to give me another mountain to start climbing. Remember that come-to-Jesus meeting Tanner had with me. God would give us a baby when He was ready. I still don't like those meetings, because I am usually wrong about something. I don't like to be confronted; none of us do. I had come to the point in life where I said, "Okay, God, I have plenty to handle with Tanner, and maybe I just need to focus more on him and not another baby."

Two weeks later, in the middle of the night, we got a call from the agency. Ironically the birth mom who wanted to talk to us lived ten minutes from our house. Okay, this was weird. We are both dealing with an agency in California and we lived in the same city. Needless to say, I got no sleep the rest of the night. I called her the next day. We talked about us living near each other, but she reassured us she wanted no contact after the baby was born. With Tanner we had a semi-open adoption and sent letters/pictures. In her situation, she wanted us to not exist.

We met each other. She was due in eight weeks, and she had an eight-month-old baby. We could understand why she wouldn't want to raise two that close together. Now I have got to be very careful what I say here. Let's just say she knew the system well. We took her to a doctor since she had not had any prenatal care. She was four centimeters, and I finally did enough begging that the doctor agreed to induce her.

Troy and I were both there for the ultrasound. We thought for sure we were going to have another boy. His name would be Tucker Robert, named after Troy's dad, Bob. Well, we were shocked to find out we were going to have a daughter. Down deep, I think I was really hoping for a girl. I wanted to buy dresses, bows, and dollies. I called my mom and she said, "We have got to come up with a girl's name." We had to stick with the T theme. I just love a theme! She had heard on a talk show the name Tiana. I threw it at Troy, and he actually liked the name, so Tiana Michaela she would be. Michaela was after my dad, Mike. At 5:30 that night, our baby entered the world. Many prayers were sent to heaven, and God gave us an angel!

We quickly took her out of the room at the birth mom's request. The hospital let us stay in a private room. The first time we adopted, the hospital wasn't very accommodating to us. They don't have many adoption births. I threw a little stink, and this time they were overly nice. I guess they remembered us! We were so thrilled to have our beautiful baby in our arms. She had dark hair and big brown eyes. She still does. I instantly put a pink bow in her hair. Good thing she had hair. She didn't sleep much that night, but that was okay. We just wanted to hold her.

The next day the attorney met us once again for the signing of paperwork. Right before we met with him, we were hit with some valuable information. The birth mom confessed to taking drugs during the whole pregnancy. Our little angel was a crack cocaine baby. We had a decision to make—keep her, even though she would have a lot of issues in the days, months, and years to come, or let her go. We had no doubts. This was our baby no matter what. God would not give us more than we could handle.

The paperwork was signed, and things were not left on a very good note with the birth mom and us. We know she still lives in our city, and we know she is still on drugs; we also know she knows where we are. Enough said about all of that. We were taking our little baby girl home!

Tanner loved her from the beginning and played big brother to the hilt. He was a little upset that she couldn't play trucks with him and that she cried a lot. I do mean a lot! She did not like to be held, she did not like the swing, she did not like the bouncy seat, and she did not like life. Troy and I both looked at each other, and we both knew mountains were forming. Our pediatrician put her on Benadryl to help with the drug withdrawals. I was so young and really kind of dumb back then. I thought our life was going to be great. I thought we would dress our kids up cute and go places all the time. We chose to stay home instead.

Tiana hated commotion and still does. She just cried and cried. I felt like a failure again. She was not a sleeper. By this time, I had not slept through the night in four years. I was so tired, I was stressed, and I was depressed. I wanted to be so happy, but I just couldn't. The whys came rushing around me again, but I had to keep trusting God. He was not going to give me more than I can handle, but I really needed a break. Someone actually told me, "This is what you get when you adopt and don't have your own baby." There it was again—the cruel words of others telling me we were suffering because of sin in our life. I really have issues with this.

My mom would come over every day and help with laundry. She loves to do laundry, and I hate it. She still comes over and does laundry. If Mama's happy, everybody is happy, so she keeps washing our clothes! Tanner would also entertain my mom. Remember, he is a talker. Tiana only wanted me, and most of the time I wasn't good enough for her either. She did love her paci. I was so glad. She actually used her paci until she turned three. Don't tell her pediatrician this! One day she just decided she was done with the paci and threw it in the trashcan. I made a big deal about what a big girl she was, and then when she wasn't looking, I dug it out of the trash! I just knew it would be a horrible night without her paci, but it wasn't. For the next year, every time she saw a trash truck she would say, "Bye, bye, paci."

She was adorable. After the first eight months of her life, she did mellow out some. I knew there would be problems in the future, but as of right then, I could handle life. Tanner and Tiana were buddies. She loves books. She would read them to her dollies. She had a very special doll and named him Ralphie. I had an Uncle Ralph who was bald just like this baby, thus the name Ralphie. Once, Tanner shoved Ralphie in the back of his toy semi-truck. She cried and cried. He made better choices, the next time and gave her dollies rides in his dump trucks so they could see.

She mimicked everything he did. They kept me on my toes all day and night; still do. She often asks, "How am I supposed to go to sleep if only one eye is tired?" She is my little singer. I have videos of Tiana singing her heart out. Her speech has always been very hard to understand, and one day she was singing. "I read about it in the booger ation, you read it too." Finally figured it out: "I read about it in the book of Revelation, you read it too." I had to rock her to sleep each night and sing songs—many verses of songs. When she moved out of the Winnie the Pooh nursery, she got my old furniture set. Daddy painted the walls blue, and I got busy decorating my little angel's room.

When my dad died, I started collecting angels. I hung all 258 of them all over her room. You know what Tiana told me? She said she couldn't sleep because the angels sang too loud. She was never a good sleeper and was getting worse, so I thought maybe they were just too much. I put them in totes for the attic and made her room a princess theme. She still didn't sleep. By age four, we were really starting to see some issues with Tiana. In kindergarten, she was also diagnosed with bipolar disorder. But that wasn't all. She has extreme anxiety, ADHD, and OCD.

The waves were crashing again. Life was falling apart, my depression had deepened, and where was God? He was right there beside me, helping me climb back up. I think Tiana has been invited to only three parties in ten years. I understand why she isn't, but she doesn't understand that she is different. She gets really frustrated with school, people, and life. Most days she pushes all my buttons, and that is not a good thing. Other days she is the most well-behaved, loving little girl. The whole bipolar illness really confuses me as I watch it unfold. She is a drama queen, maybe because of the entire princess stuff in her room, and she thinks she is now a queen! In that case, I need to put the angels back up.

Getting dressed for the day is a major issue for Tiana. She recently got an IEP at school and is starting to go to special education. My kids just need extra help. Their illness isn't their fault. I will continue to be their biggest cheerleader in life. We have a sticker chart on the refrigerator. If everybody has twenty stickers by the end of the week, we do a fun family activity. Just putting a bowl in the sink earns a sticker, because they really don't have a concept of life skills. Our goals for Tanner and Tiana are to love Jesus and learn how to do basic life skills.

The school staff has been absolutely wonderful for us, kind of like a second family. While at school, a few kids have befriended Tiana, and that means so much to us. A lot of people in society turn away from special needs kids. That is so sad. She has a love for horses. We are members of a ranch, and the family feeds them on the weekend—the family being everybody but me. This city slicker needs her beauty sleep! We donated a Clydesdale to be used at the ranch, and of course we stuck with the T theme again. Thunder is known as the gentle giant! There is definitely a connection between horses and special needs kids. Tiana feels loved and accepted with her horse friends. I wish I could take all the heartache away, but I can't. Tiana is my hero. She has had a hard ten years, but no matter what, she will always be my little angel.

"Heroes" is a fantastic song written about special needs kids. They all are true heroes.

Chapter 6

My Little Miracle

Tessa Jo

Remember that 1 percent chance of ever having a baby of our own? Well, here is her story. I was craving McDonald's double cheeseburgers, and I hate meat. After two nights of Troy having to go get me my fix, he stopped at Walgreens and bought a pregnancy test. I had taken many of them over the years, and it was always negative. Well, he was determined I was pregnant. He said, "Go take the test right now." I said, "I'll take it in the morning." Well, he is a pacer and wouldn't stop until I went to the bathroom. Before I even flushed, the test showed positive.

Tanner and Tiana were fighting in the toy room and I went to show Troy the test. He turned white and grabbed the car keys. I said, "Where are you going?" He said, "Back to Walgreens. I'm going to buy a double pack just to make sure." We were both very much in shock and thought for sure it was a mistake, but after three positive results, we called the doctor. It was confirmed. We were pregnant! When we told people, nobody believed us. Some people actually thought we meant our dog was going to have a puppy!

For the first few months I felt fine, as long as I had my double cheeseburgers! After about four months, I started having really high blood pressure. My doctor sent me to a specialist, and the specialist sent me to more specialists. I was in and out of the hospital a lot. You know it's bad when they wrap your bed railings with towels in case you have a seizure. I was put on bed rest. That is when Tiana learned many songs! She would crawl up beside me and sing and read. By now I was diagnosed with pre-eclampsia.

We only had one Christmas tree up that year. It came to the point where I was not allowed out of bed except to go to the bathroom. Troy would bring both kids into our room for picnic meals! He can be creative. I sent out our Christmas card, letter, and picture and was really hoping our baby and I could make it until my due date of March 5. I knew down deep I never would. My goal was Valentine's Day, but that didn't happen either.

I was admitted into the hospital on December 15, 2003. By the way, all three of our kids were born in the same hospital. They all have different parents, and we love them all the same. Just a little side note to share! We were informed that an emergency c-section would be performed in the morning. Nothing was getting my blood pressure down. This was a very scary time for us. I was in danger, but our baby was really in danger. We found out it was better to have a premature girl than a premature boy. Girls develop a little faster. Girls rule, boys drool—at least that is the saying at our house.

The NICU nurse came and explained what would be happening after the birth. Well, that really scared us, and we called Aunt Caro. She is a retired nurse and knows everything about medical stuff! She said, "I'm on my way." We didn't know until later, but she had her bags packed for weeks because she had a feeling this would happen. Grandma and Pop had our kids to deal with, and Aunt Caro, Troy, and I were watching the *Survivor* finale in my hospital room. What a long night. Talk about the what ifs. My mind was flooded with questions, and I was really worried.

Tessa Jo Patterson was born at 9:35 a.m. the next day and whisked off to the NICU. She was sixteen inches long and weighed two pounds and fifteen ounces. Our little miracle had arrived with many tubes and machines. Someday she would be home with us, and that would make us sing! We had a big mountain ahead of us while she fought for her life. We were not allowed to hold her because she was so small, had so many machines, and she could easily bruise. I would go down to the

NICU in the middle of the nights and put my fingers through the little holes on the tent covering her bed. I remember crying and crying.

I was so depressed. What have I done to my little baby? Why couldn't I have kept her in me longer? Why does God allow suffering? I felt like I was to blame for all of this suffering. Once again those words said to me after my dad's death came to my mind: "Only people with sin in their lives have bad things happen to them." I knew that wasn't true, but I doubted myself a lot.

Aunt Caro was our rock to lean on during this time. I have had to do two really hard things in life. One was watching my dad take his final breath. The second was leaving the hospital without my baby. Tessa was a fighter—still is. On Christmas we got to finally hold her. We put her Christmas stocking beside her and took our first family picture. Every day we went back and forth to the hospital. That was really hard to do since Tanner was six and Tiana was two and a half, but we did it. Troy was plowing snow at the time and would go feed her bottles in the middle of the night. I would go in the morning while Tanner was at kindergarten and Tiana was at Grandmas. Then when Troy came home from work in the afternoon, we would all go be with Tessa.

The kids loved putting their hands through the holes and petting their new baby. After forty days, she came home weighing four pounds and three ounces. She was hooked to a heart monitor at all times. When the monitor would go off, that meant she wasn't breathing. It was not a quiet sound either. It was ear splitting. I remember the first time it went off in the middle of the night. Troy fell out of bed. It's funny now but was so scary at the time.

Tessa was a good baby. We kept her in her room a lot so she wouldn't get germs, and we had a special heater to keep her warm. Soon after she came home, there was a big snowstorm, so I was left as a single mother with three kids. Good thing Grandma and Pop are only two miles away! Tessa had to get a lot of therapy to catch up to her real age. By the age of one, she was off the charts on height and weight. She still is! Poor little thing is built like her daddy. She has big feet and is very tall.

Tessa has brought so much joy to our lives. This was a hard time for us because Tanner was diagnosed as bipolar when she was just a few months old. I just kept telling myself, *God will never give me more than I can handle, but I could use a little break.* I was a busy mommy with a tiny preemie, a three-year-old girl, and a little boy who had just been diagnosed with a serious mental illness. Looking back, I don't know how I did all I did. I always planned great birthday parties for each of them. The house was always clean and picked up. It still is. I have issues! I felt like super-mommy, but inside I was mad at God. I dreamed about a normal life, and it was not looking good.

Tessa loved her paci, but she had to be different and call it boppie. Boppie went everywhere with her. She was good too. She could twirl it in her mouth without using her hands and even talk with it in her mouth. She was always very verbal and still is. You don't ruffle up her feathers. She lets you know! The things she says crack me up. My days are absolutely crazy, but I wouldn't change them. Well, I might change the bipolar rages going on, but that would be the only change.

Tessa has long blonde hair, and I love to deck my girls out. We have piles of bows, piggies, and headbands. I thought we would all be girly girls, but Tessa switches back and forth. Sometimes her favorite pair of shorts and a T-shirt is good enough for the whole week. Other times, every hair, every piece of clothing, and her nails have to be perfect. Daddy is the official nail painter in our home. Those big mitts can do some good painting! I'm just sayin'. One time he let Tessa paint his toenails. I have pictures!

Tessa loves to cook with me. Both girls do, but I try to have them take turns. Tessa is a mini me. She wants to take care of everybody and not have anybody upset. She already is taking medicine for acid reflux, so I am sure ulcers will be coming soon. I have panic attacks, and one time I was taking the kids to a playground. Yep, I get panic attacks even going to a playground. Anyway, she asked me for a Tic-Tac out of my purse. I thought that was strange but gave her one. A few minutes later she said, "Now, I am much better since I took my panic pill." Poor thing!

All our kids love to be outside. We live outside. Even in the winter I bundle them up and go outside. Tessa, age seven, already has a boyfriend. His name is Parker. Our girls, Parker, and his sister, Kaylee, house hop. The four of them are great buddies. We are so thankful they accept our kids for who they are, not what they have. They play together all the time. I really hope Parker and Tessa do end up together. Then I will definitely have to write another book.

Let me tell you about Halloween at our house. We are fall people. We decorate with pumpkins, gourds, and scarecrows, not so much the scary stuff. Anyway, we have a rule at our house. Actually Amy, a friend who was killed in a horrible car accident, came up with this rule, and we honor it. We go trick or treating until their buckets are full. We come home, and they have five minutes to eat as much candy as they can. After the five minutes, the rest gets sent to work with Daddy. Bipolar disorder and sugar are not a good mix. I'm just sayin'!

Anyway, the kids categorize all their candy into piles, and the timer starts! Tanner eats everything sour; remember, he is a strange eater. Tiana eats all the chocolate. That's my girl! Tessa picks a sucker. Are you serious? Finally this year, she caught on. She devours all her favorites and leaves the sucker for the last minute. We have the years on video. Oh my, precious memories! Tessa likes the social part of school, but the work is hard for her. The NICU doctors and nurses often said preemies have trouble with learning disabilities. I don't even want to think of another mountain to climb.

Tessa is a singer. We have listened to many of her concerts. She is a mother hen to Tanner and Tiana. She sticks up for them at all times. Tessa is an absolute joy to be with, but she hates shopping. That is a hard thing for me to handle. A few years ago, she climbed up on my lap and said, "I know I was in your tummy, but thanks for badopting me too." She is growing up way too fast. Tessa has to put up with a lot, and I mean a lot, with special needs siblings. I get really down about this. The verbal abuse I receive really hurts, and I can't even imagine what it does to her. I know they don't mean what they say, and we forgive them, but it is sometimes hard to forget. I am interested to see how Tessa will grow up. She is one of a kind! One of her favorite songs is "Butterfly Fly Away." I think Daddy and Tessa should sing it as a duet at her wedding someday! She is my little miracle.

I never want any of my kids to grow up, but I know someday I will have to let my butterflies fly away.

Chapter 7

Raising the Rafters

I lived in the same house for twenty years. Troy didn't; they moved often. When we were engaged, we had a starter home built. I decorated the kitchen with apples because the name of our road was Sweet Cider. Isn't that the cutest name? We brought Tanner home to our little house and shared many great memories. When he was three, we had our dream home built. I love every part of decorating: the planning, picking the colors, buying items, hammering many nails into the walls. I just love it all!

This was the house we were going to retire in—at least that was our plan. We brought Tiana home to this house. I also was not feeling too great during this time. We didn't know if it was because of her crankiness or something else. We soon found black mold growing in our home. The house had been built too low to the ground and the yard was graded too high. Our basement was full of mold, and so was our foyer. I was tested for allergies and found out I was very allergic to this particular kind of mold. We fought with the builder, to no avail.

I sank into deep depression again. This was our dream home, it was decorated perfectly, and it was beautiful, but it was making me sick. It turned into a devastating problem, and we ended up selling it "as is" and losing a lot of money. We had our possessions professionally cleaned at a mold company. Some things had to be thrown away. I was so lethargic and sick. Before moving, I ruptured two discs in my neck and had to have surgery. We had no home, so we moved in with Grandma and Pop! Tanner was five, and Tiana was one. They had their hands full while Troy went to work and I sat in the recliner with pain pills. We lived with them for one hundred days. Now you just can't do that with everybody!

Pop actually found us an existing house to buy while on a bike ride. Thinking back, he rode his bike a lot during this time. Probably for peace and quiet! We ended up buying that fixer upper. Troy is not a handyman, but he can paint. It is amazing what a gallon of paint can do. I told him the kitchen was going to be red with green cabinets. He just said, "Yes dear." Now I know what you all are thinking—that sounds really ugly. It isn't! Our kitchen has just the right shades of colors to be perfect. We have a big country-style kitchen that holds a lot of people. After new appliances, lots of paint, and an apple border (the apple theme moved to each home), I am able to cook lots of good food.

We made the front fancy living room into a toy room. The walls are painted to look like logs, and there is a picket fence in the doorway. No toys can pass the gate! We made the dining room into our computer/sitting room. While writing this book, I have spent a lot of time in there. There is a sign hanging over the desk that says, "God will never give me more than I can handle." Our bedroom was lavender with pink drapes. Troy didn't think he could sleep with those colors looking at him, so he painted the walls a goldish color. Our bathroom had big gray lily pad wallpaper. We started scraping off wallpaper when we got possession of the house, and more gold paint was added.

Daddy did something special in Tiana's room. He gave her light blue walls with white, fluffy clouds. Tanner's room was painted the color of dirt, and he had construction trucks everywhere. It is now dark gray and filled with stuffed husky dogs. Tessa's room is green with ladybugs, but she is feeling the urge to remodel. In our great room we have a hundred-year-old door hanging up high. Troy said,

"Yes, dear" again! Anyway, the sign on the door says, "a house is built with boards and beams; a home is built with love and dreams."

We were sad to leave our dream house, but we realized a house really doesn't make a home. The people who live inside are what matters. We also changed some wallpaper and carpet. We had a new roof put on, a new air conditioner/furnace added, pulled out the old shrubs, and put new landscaping in. Our windows starting leaking, and we even put new windows in. I got panes, or the technical word is muttons. Our original windows were just big and plain. I often said I was going to put masking tape squares in them so they looked like panes. Once again, our luck was rotten. Our windows had literally rotted the front walls of our house and we had to have all the brick, studs, and drywall taken off and rebuild. Not a cheap fix.

We decided we didn't want to move again. Every time we moved, we had another kid! We brought Tessa home to this house, and we were done! So we took out a big loan and remodeled. All the siding had to go too, so we decided to really change the look of our beige house. I wanted a primitive yellow (mustard), and Troy wanted barn red (ketchup). We compromised, mixed the colors together, and got taco sauce. Actually it is called terra cotta. We are now known as the orange house. At least we are known in the neighborhood—although sometimes people go inside when we come out. We have two black rockers on our front porch. We will still be rocking forty years from now, because that is how long it will take to pay the loan off. We are really just passing through life and waiting for our heavenly home. Can you imagine what heaven will be like? When we stand in His presence there really will be no place like home.

I can't wait to *see* how beautiful and peaceful heaven will be! "I Can Only Imagine."

Chapter 8

Plowing through the Snow

Troy Lee

Where do I begin with this chapter? I love Troy with all my heart. He is a positive person, and I am negative. He can't keep surprises, and I can save them for a year. He builds me up when I am down; I build him up when he is down. We share a lot of the same illnesses. I have stomach ulcers and acid reflux, and now he has acid reflux. I think it is the food he eats and Gas-X pills he takes, but I am not a doctor, just a wife! We both have sleep apnea. Yep, our bedtime is real romantic. Kiss, I love you, put on your mask! We both suffer with depression. However, God is good. He never lets us battle depression at the same time. Can you imagine if we did?

Troy is also really smart. He learned something early in our marriage from Christian comedian Jeff Allen. He asked himself two questions. Do I want to be right, or do I want to be happy? He hasn't been right in ten years, but he is a happy, happy man. His life saying is, "Happy wife, happy life." I picked a winner! We make a good team.

Actually, we are both training for a mini marathon. Our team name is Puffin Pattersons. *I think I can, I think I can, I think I can.* Actually, that is what we say each day as we struggle to be the best parents possible for our kids. Troy cracks me up. I have a lot of laughs just watching him. I have issues, but he really has issues. He likes routine. I can't make new recipes. He's a meat and potatoes kind of a guy.

By the time he gets to bed at night, I am just exhausted by his routine. First of all, he is a sweetheart. After we get the kids to bed, he pushes our recliners up to the TV so I can see. We watch a show from our DVR. We don't do well with commercials. They take up too much time. We are not patient people! After we watch our show, he takes the dog outside. We never had another boy, so we named our dog our other boy name, Tucker Robert. Then Troy takes his medication and drinks a full glass of water. He actually follows the rules on the prescriptions (not me!), and then he begins his lockdown system. The patio door is locked and shaken to make sure it is secure. The door to our garage is locked and chained, the computers are turned off, the front door is locked and chained, and the outside lights are turned off and back on again to make sure they work.

Then he sets the security system. It beeps for thirty seconds, and Tucker barks every time. Then Troy moves Tucker's cage into our bedroom so Tucker won't be lonely in the kitchen. Troy then proceeds to kiss the kids good night. He starts with Tanner, who is usually buried under the covers, and then he moves to Tessa. The girls switch beds at night. Tessa likes the full-size bed; Tiana likes the feel of the twin size with a railing. I don't care where they sleep, as long as I get my beauty sleep. So he kisses Tessa good night. She is like a snow angel every night, all spread out with no covers. She is a little furnace like her daddy. Then he kisses Tiana, but Tiana is not a sound sleeper, and five nights out of the seven she wakes up and looks at him. This makes him yell, and the dog barks again.

He finally comes into our room, uses the bathroom, and then comes to bed. Before he lies down, he has to drink another glass of water, and he can't swallow until he is lying on his pillows. If I ask him a question and he swallows too early, he has to do it again. Am I right about the issues!

There are times when I am mean and hide around the corners and scare him. I know his routine; I know where he will be at any given time. He gets mad when I do this, but sometimes I just need to laugh. I don't tell you all this to make you think he is weird; I tell you his routine so you will understand my life better. A few years ago, Troy was diagnosed with bipolar disorder. Yep, you have added right: three bipolar people in one house.

I saw the signs and knew the diagnosis was coming, but I tried to make bargains with God. If Troy can be normal, I will pray more. If Troy, can be normal, I will read the Bible more. If Troy can be normal, I will be a better wife. Well, the bargaining didn't work, and once again, life fell apart. This was going to be a huge mountain to get over.

In 1999, Troy's dad, Bob, died of a sudden massive heart attack at the age of fifty-two. Bob and Troy were a lot alike. They both drove trucks, they both had Patterson tempers, and they even had the same receding hairline. Many times Troy wishes he could talk work with his dad. My father- in-law had a sense of humor and enjoyed picking on me. I used to think he really didn't like me, but he reassured me by saying he only picks on people he loves. Well, I must have really been loved.

He invented the come-to-Jesus meetings, as you know, but he also had another trademark—the sniff. He would be rambling on about something, totally catch me off guard, and say, "You know what I mean, *sniff*." I would reply, "Yes, sir." He would get the biggest laugh over this. Oh I miss him, but I am so glad my husband has a lot of his qualities.

For years Troy drove a semi. He would leave at 3:30 a.m. We are early to bed, early to rise people. Well, not so much me. I am not a morning person, but everyone else in this house is. They are all so chipper, too. I needed him at home more, so he got a job at the state highway department in the maintenance section. He fixed roads and picked up dead deer in the summers. Great supper conversations, by the way! In the winters he plowed snow. They are on call from November 1 to April 1. I was basically a single mother with three kids.

He loved driving the big trucks with his buddy Jamie. There are no words to describe Jamie! I'm just sayin'! After about six years of plowing, Troy got a promotion and is now the traffic operation manager. He is in charge of signs and lines and doesn't plow snow, except for fun. Troy developed heart problems. I really do think I am too much for him! He had two heart surgeries, and after the last procedure, he developed narcolepsy. Narcolepsy is when you have sleep seizures. You just fall asleep no matter what you are doing or where you are going. I have seen it happen. He was reading a book to Tiana, and all of a sudden was out. This also happened when he was driving until the rumble strips woke him up. He had to be put on medication for this illness and was no longer able to have a license to drive big trucks.

This was going to be another big mountain to climb, but God had done some of the walking for us. Troy's new position didn't require a commercial driver's license, so his job was not in jeopardy. We were very thankful since he carries our health insurance. The narcolepsy medicine is very expensive, but the bipolar prescriptions are outrageous. Walgreens greets us by our first names! Yep, they really do!

Over the years, I have spent a lot of time in emergency rooms with Troy. His heart goes out of rhythm and he has to get it pumping right again. He also has a partially prolapsed mitral valve. I have seen him be shocked. I have seen an entire staff in his room frantically working on him. I have seen him minutes away from dying. I never want to lose him. Without Troy beside me, I would really fall apart. We just fit together, and I will forever love him. Life is a lot like a snowstorm. We are always trying to plow through, although in our home, we mostly have blizzards. We have no idea what the future holds, but God does. Once again, He will never give me more than I can handle. My dream came true, I have the "bestest" husband in the world! We have gone through a lot together, more than most couples ever face in a life time. "Through It All" we have learned to trust not only in each other but also in God.

I thank God for the mountains, for the valleys, and for the storms He has brought us through. I could go on about Troy's morning routine, but I will stop. Maybe in my sequel!

Chapter 9

As the Stomach Churns

Twila Jo

D o you ever wish you could just run away? I do, often. I would go to the ocean, but I can't even drive myself to the grocery store, let alone to the ocean. I guess it is time to tell you about me. I don't like to talk about myself, but sometimes things have to be said. As you know, I battle depression every day, sometimes every minute, and sometimes even every second. I hate it. I don't want to be like this, but hearing what my kids say during rages makes my depression worse. For over twenty years I have been taking medication. I also developed my first stomach ulcer when I was in second grade. I couldn't do those time tests fast enough. I also have thyroid issues. Why do we even have a thyroid? I have panic attacks and take amazing little pills for that!

For years I didn't feel well. Early in 2009, I became very sick. I ended up in the hospital for a week with double pneumonia, very low hemoglobin and iron, thyroid out of whack, and major stomach problems. I was also having blurred vision and figured it was time for bifocals. I had hit forty and was falling apart. I remember telling Troy that I felt like I had just celebrated my last Christmas. I really thought I was dying. I had no energy couldn't do any of the normal "mommy" chores. My mom came over when Troy left for work and stayed until he came home. I slept a lot. She completely took care of everything. That is when her hair definitely needed to be colored more often!

I went to lots of specialists, and every one of those doctors would find something else wrong with me. I had c-difficule, MRSA, erosive gastritis, diabetes, lots of allergies, and the list goes on and on. It's a long story I really don't want to focus on, but I ended up at Mayo Clinic. My mom and Pop took all of us on the Mayo trip. They watched the kids at the hotel while Troy took me to doctors' appointments and waited while I had many tests done.

The doctors there told me my body was shutting down and I was dying. However, the good news was that they could help me get better. It was such a relief to know there really was something wrong with me, that my pitiful mind wasn't making it up, and that I would eventually feel better. I was being overmedicated with steroids for Cushing's disease, which I never had. I had to slowly go off this medication. The bone pain was indescribable. It was not going to be an easy journey. Remember, God will never give me more than I can handle. Well, this was another one of those give-me-a-break times. I feel like I missed a lot of our kids' toddler years because I just didn't feel good.

By now, I had developed more ulcers; gee, I wonder where Tessa gets it from. I am a worrier. I worry before there is even anything to worry about. I am always sorry for things I can't even control. My mom often jokes around with me and calls me Twila Sorry instead of Twila Patterson. Well, I was worried in 2009. I was checked for four different kinds of cancers. I had many surgeries and procedures, and I was falling apart. I gained a considerable amount of weight. I was exhausted, and I couldn't even function. My mom really was super-grandma!

While at Mayo, I also saw the retina specialist team. A few weeks before we left for Mayo, I was told why my vision was so blurry, but the diagnosis didn't really hit me until I was at mayo. I was diagnosed with Bilateral Idiopathic Juxtafoveal telangiectasis. This is a very rare eye disease that usually affects men in their seventies and usually affects only one eye. I am a woman, I am forty, and I have the disease in both eyes. I began asking why again. What are you thinking, God? Do I not have enough to deal with? I had lots of questions, and I still do. I was devastated as I listened to the third retina specialist I had seen in three days. He explained there was no cure. The only thing that could be done was experimental; there were no guarantees. I was slowly losing my sight and would eventually only be able to see shadows.

These were the words that were crashing like waves in my mind weeks before leaving for Mayo. I had the mayo specialist team give a fourth opinion, and they agreed with the other three doctors. Then the diagnosis really hit me. The plan was and still is to this day to have painful eye injections every five weeks for the rest of my life. Now there are older people who get shots in their eyes and have no problems, but I am here to tell you my injections are different. I was really discouraged and thought I must be a wimp. My specialist explained it to me, and I finally got it. The younger the eye, the more sensitive the injections. My fate is determined at each appointment.

As of right now the shots are keeping the vision I do have, but the blood cells are very damaged in my eyes and they are dying off, which is not good. My vision is blurry at all times, and it is very hard to focus. I lost my license over a year ago, my independence is gone, and my ability to have a job is impossible. However, I can't get social security assistance because I am not totally blind. That's why I am writing! Maybe my book sales will buy groceries for this gang! While I worked on this book, I typed with my eyes closed or squinted. I have started wearing dark glasses if there is any light shining.

Each of my family members really helps me in his or her own way. All curbs and steps should be marked with a lot of bright yellow paint. I'm just sayin'! I know a lot of people by their voices. It is true; when one of the senses goes, the others kick it into high gear. My life is not what I had planned. I stay at home a lot. It is just easier than trying to go somewhere. Some days my eyes really hurt. Some days my vision is worse than other days. Some days the pressure in my eyes is so high that I just want to take my eyeballs out and set them on the nightstand. I have trouble sleeping at night because I am worried I will wake up with no sight. I told you, I am a worrier!

There are so many things I want to do before I can't do them anymore. Troy is so patient with me. I feel like my life is getting very small. I really want to get my story out before I am no longer able. If it ever gets published, that will be great. Oh, I guess that happened since you are reading it! The past two years have been very depressing. I feel all alone. I never know when my eyesight will take a turn for the worse. I live each day leaning on God. It is very hard raising two special needs kids who need so much extra attention. Living with three bipolar people in one house is very stressful. I invite people to spend a day in my life, but nobody ever comes!

Music has always been a huge part of my life, but now it is my life. Troy took me to a concert with our favorite singers, Ernie Haase and Signature Sound. We got there three hours before the doors opened so we could get a front-row seat. I wanted to *see* them one more time. Those are my boys! Music does a lot for me. You can't even imagine the struggles that are placed in front of me each day. They aren't little hills either; they are mountains. I don't say all this to have a pity party. I am just sharing with you my life and how I want God to use me to help others. The song "You Raise Me Up" just rings in my ears.

Maybe I should have made an audio book so you could all hear what I hear. Lord, "You Raise Me Up" so I can stand on mountains.

Chapter 10

Twila's Treasures

On March 21, 1990, my dad surprised me by creating business cards for me. He knew I was crafty and wanted me to pursue this dream. I didn't take the time to really thank him that night, and I will always regret this. The next day was the gas explosion at ZIP. It took me almost twenty years to finally let the loss go and to start over. On the day of the explosion, there was Styrofoam and material blowing all around the ashes. Nobody knew what it was, but I did. I had made wreaths, and Dad had put them on a table by the front window of the shop. He was selling my treasures for me. I didn't just lose my dad that day. I also lost the dream of ever creating my own business. I gave up.

However, after a lot of struggling with doubt, I am proud to say that in November 2009, my dream came true. I opened Twila's Treasures for two days a week out in our garage. Now the garage gets transformed each November to look like a winter wonderland store. I buy items all year and then create treasures the week before the sale. There are lots of primitives and old-fashioned, country treasures. You have to know what grungy and grubby mean in order to appreciate my sale! My friend Janice taught me all about those words!

I went into this with one goal—well, really two goals. The first goal was to honor my dad with the dream he shared with me, and the second was not go into debt. I haven't made much of a profit, but I am not out any money for what I do. My husband is very patient as he hangs white sheets all around the perimeter of the garage, sets up tables, and brings all the treasures down from the attic.

Our attic is incredible. It is categorized by season or event. Yep, I have issues. Anyway, a few years ago we needed more flooring up in the attic. You will understand why when you read the Christmas chapter! Troy carried all the plywood up the wood steps and was going to make me a bigger attic. Happy wife, happy life! The kids were in bed, one night, I was watching decorating shows on TV, and Troy was in the attic working. I heard a big thud but didn't think much about it until he had been up in the attic for an hour. I was getting mad that the flooring was taking so long, and just as I was about to go and start yelling, he came walking in very slowly. He sat in his recliner and just looked at me.

I said, "Is there a problem?"

He replied, "I just fell through the ceiling and was hugging a beam in between my legs for the last forty-five minutes."

I did what every other loving wife would do. I ran into the garage to determine the damage, and then I gave him a bag of frozen veggies for his pain. Needless to say, the flooring did not get done for several months. I have to say something here. You would think this would be one of those big life lessons to learn from. Well, several months later he went to the attic to finish the flooring and fell through again, but this time it was just his work boot. Remember, he doesn't have feet; he has skis. I just shook my head in disbelief that another huge hole had been made. Not Troy—he was proud that he caught himself before going all the way down! I guess in his mind he did learn a lesson from the first fall. I keep thinking of the song "Love Lifted Me" as I write this. Troy must really love me! My uncles, Loren and Jim, came and fixed the two holes, and there will be no more flooring added, ever. That was stated in a come-to-Jesus meeting by both of us.

Okay, back to my winter wonderland garage. I even put fake snow all over the floor, and Troy doesn't ask me why. He is one smart man. Did I pick a good one or what!

Just a side note—he also busted an attic step on one of his many trips up and down. For months we would jump over the missing step until it just got too dangerous. Now we have metal ones. "Love Lifted Me." I'm just sayin'!

Chapter 11

Christmas!

I live for the fall and winter. My life revolves around Christmas. I love all the planning and preparing for this special time of year. In September, I wrap all the Christmas gifts. I know, issues! They are stacked in a corner and look so pretty just waiting to be placed under the trees. In October, I do anything ahead of time that I can possibly do. I am a room mom at school and have parties to plan, so I get that all done. I also am the WWWW (wacky winter wonderland woman). I made that name up!

I am in charge of buying enough Christmas gifts for five hundred students to come shop for their families. I shop year round for this and price as I go. Jen G. happily stores all the boxes in her basement! What a friend! My mom shuttles me to every store. I love spending other people's money! I also finish any last-minute Christmas shopping and buy tons of groceries for all the things I plan on making in the weeks to come. I have lists upon lists of things that need to be completed. Christmas is coming!

Troy takes off work the first three days of November, and our home gets transformed for Christmas. On the first Sunday of December, we have our annual Christmas walk. About one hundred people come walking through our house to look at all our trees, eat lots of homemade goodies, and visit. You see, I can't be normal and just put one tree up. We put up twelve trees! I know, I have issues! Troy is the official tree builder and branch spreader. I do the lights and decorations. We have a system, and it works! It is crazy at our house, but if we get everything done in those three days, we celebrate with the Pizza Hut buffet. He does anything for food!

All the totes, boxes, sleds, snowmen, trees, etc., come down from the attic. Oh, the famous attic. It is organized chaos. Each tree has a tote. Each tote has all the lights, extras, extension cords, tree skirts, and all the ornaments for that particular themed tree. The kids' trees always go up first. Sometimes they get sneaked in the week before, but we don't turn the lights on. We don't want the neighbors to think we are weird, although I think they already know this. The kids help with their trees. Tanner's tree is decorated with husky dogs, bones, snowshoes, and a "Beware of Dog" sign. He wants to own seven real huskies someday; the neighborhood will really love us then!

Tiana's is a white tree with blue and pink lights, angels, crowns, and netting. It is a very sparkly, girly, fancy-themed tree. This is the tree most people vote as their favorite. Tessa's tree is called "Don't Get Your Tinsel in a Tangle." It is decorated with red and lime green funky ornaments and just fits her personality. You do not want to get Tessa's tinsel in a tangle. She takes matter into her own hands.

Here is a Tessa at age five story to share with you. There were some kids at school saying Tiana and Tessa weren't really sisters because they don't look alike. They often dress alike, but they look totally different. Tessa had enough and went to talk to the principal. She told her the whole story and how these girls were hurting her feelings and it needed to stop. She said, and I quote, "Just because Tiana's badopted and I'm not doesn't mean we aren't sisters. She has short brown hair I have long yellow hair, but that doesn't matter. We are sisters no matter what." That's my girl! Troy often wonders why when the kids do something good, they are my kids, and when they do something wrong, they are his kids. Why is that? 'Cause I am the mom, that's why!

Our bedroom tree is full of love, with hearts and birdhouses. The sign on our tree reads, "Meet Me under the Mistletoe." In our bathroom—yes, even the bathroom gets decorated—are clusters of greenery, smaller trees, and more birdhouses. I should state that all the twelve trees in the rooms are six to twelve feet tall. I bought a lot of them at garage sales. The trees have to pass my tests first. I sniff the branches. If it doesn't smell like smoke or mold and is $5 or less, it gets to come home with me! You never know when you might need another tree, so we always have a spare!

Now back to our house. The toy room tree is actually the tree I grew up with each Christmas. It has seen better days, but I still love it because it is full of great childhood memories. It is called, "Jingle All the Way." We decorate it with old jingle bells; there is a reason for that. If the bells are ringing, I come running because that means the kids are either fighting or throwing something. While that tree is up for two months I catch them doing lots of naughty things. They still have not figured out how I always know when they are in trouble. I tell them I have eyes behind my head. Tessa asked me if she was going to grow eyes behind her head when she becomes a mommy. I said, "Yep!"

The computer room tree is fancy, with one thousand white lights, gold/burgundy balls, and music ornaments. There is an angel at the top, whose little arms move back and forth. I often feel like that angel, trying to protect my family and lighting their way home. The sign on the tree says, "Peace on Earth." I just wish there was peace at home. We have a western tree in honor of Thunder. The kids help decorate this one with cowbells, rope, cowboy hats, horses, and lots of western ornaments. A piece of burlap is the tree skirt, and the sign says, "Happy Trails." I hope our kids will be able to think back on their childhood and remember the happy trails we have ridden together.

The kitchen trees, of which there are five in two clusters, are filled with red and white lights, candy canes, and gingerbread people. They are very fully decorated trees. The tree in the foyer is Troy's favorite. It is primitive and has metal buckets hanging from the branches.

The first year we put it up, several people mentioned it looked like donation baskets hanging. I thought why not! The next year I made cutesy signs that said, "Donation baskets," and people put money in them when they came to our walk. I was thinking, *This is great; we will do this every year.*

The next year, Tanner was in charge of greeting people at the front door and taking their coats. Well, we didn't know anything was going on until a good friend and relative of ours told us this story. Dave said, "Do you know Tanner is not letting people enter your house unless they put money in the foyer tree?" I was so embarrassed. He went on to mention that he told Tanner he only had a $20 bill. Tanner replied, "That is fine." The next year Tanner didn't get to be the greeter, and we didn't make much money. I have rethought that whole punishment thing through, and he will forever be the door greeter!

The front porch also has a tree full of beautiful snowflakes with a sign that says, "Welcome Flakes." There are a lot of flaky people who come to our walk, and that is why we invite them. We love them! Oh my, I nearly forgot the half tree. It really is half a tree against a wall, and it flashes red, white, and blue lights with patriotic ornaments and flags. Yes, you can really buy half trees, but they are expensive. It's kind of one of those less is more things. I was delighted to find ours at a garage sale. You should have heard the comments from Troy when I called to tell him about my wonderful half-tree find. I better not repeat them! He needed a come-to-Jesus meeting. I'm just sayin'!

My favorite tree is in the family room. It is twelve feet tall and full of all the ornaments we have collected over the years. There is no sign, there is no theme, and it is just our life nestled in a corner. I wish I could keep our life nested in a corner. I wish I could keep my kids away from hurtful situations and people, but I can't. The song "Silent Night" comes to mind right now. I wish we had peace on earth. I wish we could always have peace in our hearts, and I often wish for peace and quiet. It's a crazy life we are living. I really can't wait for heaven; there will be no more sickness, no more pain, no more sadness, and no more shame. I can't wait to hear the music in heaven, and I really can't wait to *see* my two dads, my earthly father and my heavenly Father. Wow! Jesus really is the reason for the season. "Silent Night," holy night!

PS, You are all invited to our Christmas walk. It's from 3:30 p.m. to 6:30 p.m. the first Sunday of each December! Stay three hours or three minutes. The choice is yours! We will definitely put you in the Christmas mood.

Chapter 12

Precious Memories

I honored my mom's wishes and didn't do a whole chapter on her, but I could have. Six years after my dad died, she got remarried to Jim. He is better known as Pop. At the time, it was very hard to see her with someone who was not my dad, but God has helped heal my heart. I love Pop! We are closer than I ever thought possible. He always tells me, "I don't know how you do it."

Troy and I share the challenges we are facing and the mountains we are climbing with Mom and Pop because they care. Sometimes we get together on Sunday afternoons for supper. Well, we sometimes call it lupper because it is in between the normal times for lunch and supper. Our kids don't handle commotion very well, so we go to places at abnormal times. I cherish these memories. For me, Sunday lupper marks the beginning of a new week, and I rejoice because I made it through another week. For Troy, he just likes to eat! For the kids, it is a time of making special memories with Grandma and Pop. I love my mom—I really do. She is my best friend other than Troy.

Pop and Mom have taken us on many trips over the years. Once we flew to Arizona to visit Uncle Lee and his family. We also flew to Florida to surprise Troy's brother and his family. Another time we went to Disney, where dreams really do come true. They also take us on trips to faraway doctor appointments. Troy's heart doctor is a four-hour drive one way. Mom and Pop rent an Amish hauler van, and each kid has a row to him or herself! Pop's the driver, and I get to be the navigator. I can't see a thing, but I act like I do. I don't want to get stuck in a row! Our Skittles days are over. Our trips consist of frantically trying to entertain the kids. Bipolar people have an attention span the size of a kernel of corn. Maybe I do need to feed Troy Skittles! He is a horrible pacer at airports. Note to self: pack Skittles for the next trip!

My favorite times are at the ocean with my family. My mom is going to be really mad at me for telling you this, but she will get over it! She is hilarious in the ocean waves. Hilarious! I warned Troy, but he had no idea what to expect until he saw her flailing her arms around. I am laughing just writing this. My mom loves the ocean as much as me. However, she only knows how to doggie paddle and falls over in only an inch of water. We all have seen it happen several times. The funniest part is, she can't get back up because she is laughing so hard. The more she laughs, the more Pop yells at her to get up. My kids try to help Grandma up, but she makes them fall over too.

You are probably only laughing if you know my mom, but I just had to write it! God is telling me to! She usually just sits in the sand with the water literally an inch high around her. Eventually she gets herself under control and gets into position, which is on her hands and knees. Then she starts crawling to shore. She usually goes backward. I have no idea why, but of course we all make the "beep, beep, beep" sound of a snowplow backing up. She really doesn't have far to go, and the lifeguards are usually all watching by now. She wears a white hat that always flies off her head and gets all wet. She never wears good swimsuits in the ocean because of the salt; she wears old ones that really need to be retired. My mom has issues with throwing things away. The swimsuit skirts always fly up in the air. You have to picture it with me!

She finally gets up and then has to go rest for about thirty minutes. Now you would think she would be done for the day. Nope, she comes back to the water for more. Troy and I take her out in the deep and hold her hands. She loves it out there, but we can't let go. We made that mistake once, and Pop was waving his arms on shore and the lifeguards stood up with their whistles ready. She thought she could handle it knee deep. Wrong! A big wave came, and we even warned her, but she fell over and couldn't get up. Troy went swimming and hoisted her up under her armpits. After she recovered, she actually asked Troy, and I quote, "Can we do that again? It was fun!" Are you picturing it with me? We just got back from Alabama for spring break. I have her on video! I should send it to *America's Funniest Home Videos*. It definitely would be the funniest! I can talk to my mom about anything, and she listens—usually! My dad would often tell my mom, "Why do you suppose God gave us one mouth and two ears?" I'm just sayin'! My mom has given me so many precious memories over the years. She truly is the best! My dad came from a small and very proper family. Not my mom. The Mosers are crazy, and I'm not talking mentally crazy. I am thinking of June, Vicky, (we love Luci), and Diane. Words cannot describe this family! My grandma, Linda Moser, was a wonderful lady. She had ulcers too. She worried about how my mom would entertain herself when she got older. My mom reassured her by answering, "I can rock, and I can talk." I have no further comment. I love you, Mom!

As a side note, my mom's name is Marge Zehr Bowman, but most people call her Margie. A lot of people say Tessa is a mini-Margie. Troy says, "Dear God, help me!" I guess this kind of turned into a mini-mom chapter. I could have said more, but I stopped myself. I really stopped myself! "Precious Memories," how they linger. They needed to be shared. I'm just sayin'!

Troy, Twila, Tanner, Tiana & Tessa
Tucker the dog & Thunder the Clydesdale
Happy Trails!

Little Twila

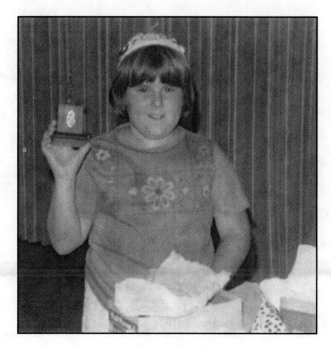

Whirlybirds

Berne Swiss Days

Graduation

Dad's printing press

Troy &Twila
For better or for worse!

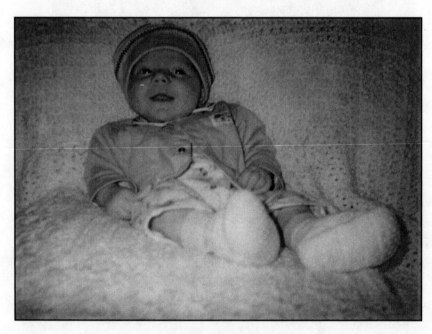

My little buddy

"Am I getting bigger?" asked Tanner.

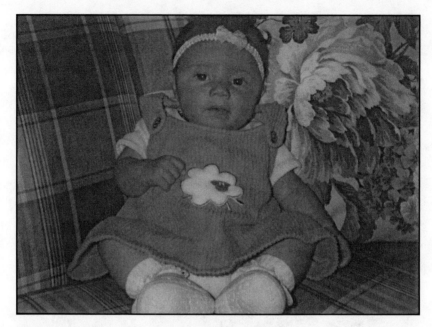

My little angel

"Princess Tiana"

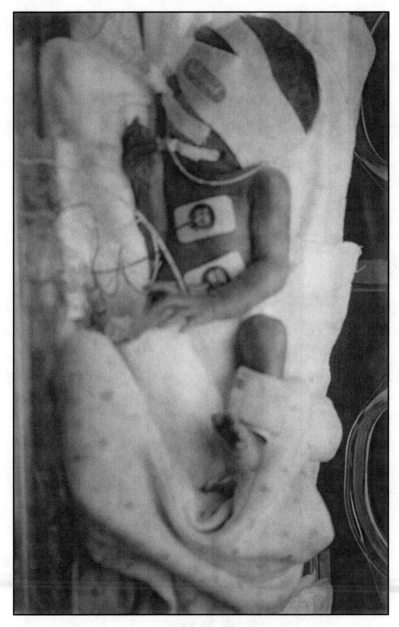

My little miracle

"I am free ears old!" Tessa said.

Rodeo time!

Our stair steps

One cowboy & two cowgirls

Merry Christmas!!!

Twila's Treasures

Grandma, Pop & our sluggers

Gulf Shores, Alabama 2011

Chapter 13

Now I See

The real reason I wanted to write this book was for my kids. I can no longer see their faces, but I hear their words and feel their hugs. I want them to remember the love that I have for each of them, the fight that I fought and am still fighting for them, and the life that we gave when we could have turned away but chose not to. I am their mommy, and I know this is God's whole plan for me. Many mountains have been climbed, and we have many more to climb. There are many more decisions and accusations to be made, and many more struggles will be fought, but I will not give up on my kids. I will not quit. There are still times when I want to run away, depression creeps in, I yell, and I am mad at God, but God always forgives and loves me no matter what. He is teaching me how to be the best mommy possible for our special kids.

Our lives are never going to be normal, but I can finally accept that. I really can accept the life God has given me. Our school motto is to do your personal best, and that is also my motto. I am not a failure as a mommy. I have been given a very hard road to travel, but I am going to make it. I am going to do my personal best! We have no idea what the future holds for our kids. Will they be able to live on their own? Will they marry? Will they be able to have jobs? Will Tanner be able to take care of his seven husky dogs? I don't have the answers, but God does, and in His perfect timing, He will share those answers with us.

Mental illness is ongoing and will never go away. Society will still continue to judge us for our parenting. Some people will continue to judge us by saying we must have sin in our lives to have so many bad things happen to us. I am here to tell you that is not true. Look at Job in the Bible. He was a man of God, but God took his life and broke it. I think God gives us hard times so we remember He is in control, not us. Each of us have our own obstacles to climb. Ours just happen to be big mountains. Why does God allow some people to suffer over and over and other people seem to have no troubles? I don't know that answer. I will ask in heaven!

I pray my family's testimony can help others facing mountains in their own lives. No more hiding behind mental illness. God can use the mountains in our lives to bring glory to Him and help others see God in all situations, good and bad. I want to stand on top of a mountain and rejoice; I am free! I don't want a pity party. I have finally accepted the life God has given me. It took me years to do this. This is definitely not what I planned for my life, and you know I am a planner. God will never give me more that I can handle. He is right beside me at every mountain, helping me climb and become a better person.

I want to be an encouragement to other families who are facing mental struggles. You are not alone. I want mental health to be treated as an illness, not a failure. And I want my husband and kids to know I love them no matter what. I don't always understand the bipolar rages, but I will always forgive and I will always love. I may not be able to physically see, but now I see the plans God has for me. I am finally free from the fear of tomorrow and from the guilt of the past. He touched me, and I'm free at last. It is a huge relief to finally accept not having a normal life. I am going to laugh more, love more, and live my life with no regrets because I finally get it. I now *see!*

I have been through a lot, but I finally get it. I don't have to be perfect. "He Touched Me," and oh the joy that floods my soul.

Chapter 14

Keep Climbing

I am not a patient person, but I am trying to work on that. I will always be a worrier, but I am trying to let the little things go by. I will always have health problems, but that is why there are Walgreens! I have a great retina specialist, even if it is scary to see a needle coming at your eye. I often hear my mom sigh when it is over. My doctor always tells me how brave I am. Then my mom takes me home and puts me to bed for twenty-four hours. I go back the next morning and do it all over again in the other eye.

I still shop; it is just a challenge now. All the soup and spaghetti cans look alike. We do once-a-month family grocery shopping. The girls cut the coupons, and I organize the lists. It takes us two hours to shop, and we walk out with three cartloads. It's a family affair! Troy is the worst shopper. Mom and Pop are great about getting the weekly stuff for us that we need to survive, like milk, eggs, juice, bread, and my M&Ms!

I still read some. I'm not really supposed to strain my eyes, but I do love a good book. I like Amish series books. There are a lot of Amish people in Berne, so I guess I relate to these books. I also get books on tape. I listen to a lot of music; it really is my life. I sing along with all my favorite groups: Signature Sound, The Hoppers, and Legacy Five. I could give you a concert in our family room! I'm just sayin'! I spend a lot of time at doctors' appointments for my kids. Their medications are constantly changing as they grow. Pop is usually my chauffer; he is a safer driver than my mom!

I still cook. Sometimes I burn things because I don't see them getting done. Sometimes I miss the whole counter and food goes flying all over the floor, but I still cook. Nothing like good Swiss cookin'. Rival Soup is my favorite. I check my email and Facebook because I have to get my chuckle for the day from Chris and Brandi, our friends from the South. After I take the kids to the bus stops in the morning, I come back to our garage and walk four miles on the treadmill. This is when I get blessed. I listen to my music and focus on having a good day and not thinking about all the whys or what ifs. I want to do everything while I still can.

I do stay home a lot. My mom takes me out on Tuesdays and Thursdays. We run some errands and eat a fish sandwich. I go to church each week. I can't see, but I can hear. I do a lot more than I am supposed to be doing. I have lists upon lists of things I want to complete before my sight is gone. How will I decorate the trees for Christmas? How will I create Twila's treasures? I can see it in my mind. My family tells me everything looks good; I hope they aren't lying! I have good days and bad days with my vision. I have more bad than good. God is preparing me.

Troy's heart is doing well as of right now. Even though all his heart problems are hereditary, he runs on the treadmill at night and is eating healthier. He is a great daddy, and the neighborhood comes alive when he drives into the garage each night. Troy is really just a big kid. I love him more and more each day. He is my rock to rest on while we are climbing the mountains. He showers me with love, and I am very blessed to call him my man! He loves his job and hopes to retire in twenty-eight more years! He would love to be able to take our family and speak at churches or events. We want to share our testimony. We really feel God is calling us to do this.

Tanner is growing into a little man but still has the mind of a little boy. His birth mom is in a mental institute, which is scary. We don't have much contact with her. Tanner is determined to work at Wendy's so he can get free food. The boy can seriously put away food! He still bangs the doorframes, checks the weather every fifteen minutes, and talks about all the NFL teams, except the Colts. He is very obsessed with certain subjects. Tanner also has conversations with the dog, and he has the dog answer him. He really has issues. Sometimes I just want to cry for him, but other times, I just have to chuckle. I think we would make a great TV show! He is a very active and talkative boy.

Tiana has a lot of issues. She is far behind her peers. She knows her birth mom took bad pills and that is why she has mental illnesses. Tiana didn't choose this life; it was given to her. She is thrilled when anybody takes the time to talk to her. She has a lot of feelings bottled up, and I hope they start pouring out soon. Life with Tiana is like riding a roller coaster. Tiana has no fear, so I guess comparing her life to a ride makes sense. She will soon begin the Special Olympics swim team. All our kids can swim well, but Tiana has a talent. When she was six she broke her wrist, and ever since then she has a trademark swim. She swims with one arm and is fast. She beats me every time, and I am really trying.

Tessa is our social butterfly and attends parties several times a month. Her schedule is so busy! During these times we do special things with Tanner and Tiana. Tessa is all about hip hop and gymnastics right now. We never know with her. Tessa is actually being checked for learning disabilities since she was so premature. I know, I am thinking the same thing ... Please, God, I really need a break. She is my little rock to lean on, and she often says, "We got to stick together, Mom." Tessa hopes to write a book and have it published someday! She doesn't understand why the ABCs aren't in order on the computer!

School is very hard for all three kids. The rages still happen. We are still keeping Walgreens in business. They each have a lot of battles to fight, but we will continue to be the best parents possible for our special kids. I already know what my sequel will be called: *The Rivers Keep Rolling*. Be watching the bookstores! Every night we watch a show as a family. It is either *Little House on the Prairie* or *Hannah Montana* reruns. I know, quite the contrast. Our favorite movie is *The Sound of Music*. All my dreams really did come true because God changed my outlook on life. Normal wasn't what He wanted for me. I like to think I am special! I am a wife and a mommy, and I am loved by God—no matter what! God is always there to help each of us climb the mountains. We just need to ask for help and lean on Him, so put your walking shoes on and start climbing!

We use to pretend we had a normal life but not anymore. I am an open book! It feels great to get it all out. I feel like a new person. I am so thankful my eyesight has stayed good enough for me to write about our life. I had to do this for myself and my family. "Climb Ev'ry Mountain" till you find your dream! I am very thankful that all my dreams have come true.

Chapter 15

A Day in the Life of the Pattersons

The first rooster awakes at 5:00 a.m. It is Tessa today. Tessa doesn't just get up by herself; she *bellers* for Daddy. I smack Troy, and he rips his mask off and goes running so her loud mouth will not wake up the other two kids. They get Tucker out of his cage. Then I go back to sleep; she didn't call my name! They proceed to let Tucker outside. Troy forgets to turn off the security system. I am glad to know it works. Of course, that commotion wakes Tiana up. I am thinking that's what he deserves, and I go back to sleep again. Tiana needs to be fed immediately upon waking. She definitely needs her morning medication right away. I'm just sayin'!

Troy sets both girls down in front of the TV with a Pop Tart, the breakfast of champions. He dozes on the couch with the dog. I get up at 6: 00 a.m., no earlier. I promptly make all the beds. I like a tidy house. I know, I have issues! I wake up Tanner. He immediately goes to the computer to check the weather. I put my exercise clothes on and go out into the family room. The TV is blaring, there are crumbs everywhere, the girls have sticky hands, and Daddy is still dozing. I smack him again! He frantically wakes up and realizes he has not taken his narcolepsy medicine yet. He quickly swallows that pill so he can be awake. Then he starts packing his lunch—another routine! I use to get up early and pack his lunch for him. It was so sweet of me, but then we had kids! I could write a whole chapter about his packing lunch routine, but I will spare you the details!

While he is doing this, I am getting the kids dressed. Of course, drama begins with Tiana. After a rage of yelling, biting, crying, and clothes flying, we are dressed. She has a lot of problems with self-esteem, which we try to build up daily. Troy goes to get dressed for work while I do the school routine. Of course, neither girl likes what the school is having for lunch today, so I have to pack their lunches. Tiana wants the same thing every time: cheese and crackers, grapes, carrots, a cookie, and a water bottle. Not Tessa; she has to be fancy. She wants a turkey sandwich with cheese, mustard, mayo, and lettuce, chips, water, a fruit cup, carrots (she doesn't eat them; it just makes me feel like a good mom), and a Rice Krispies square because she doesn't like the cookies I made.

I sign notes for each and make sure their book bags are ready. Tanner checks the TV just to make sure there are no delays. Can you believe it? We have a two-hour delay. Are you serious? I just got up for this. Troy leaves for work. The girls are still hungry, so they eat a bowl of Raisin Bran. Tanner continues to check the weather every fifteen minutes on the dot. He gives me a detailed statement every fifteen minutes. Did I mention this update happens every fifteen minutes? The kids are all off because they are out of their routine. I get the girls busy creating a craft, Tanner is pacing, and I go on the treadmill.

I am happily getting blessed with my music, thinking life is good. I will have just enough time to take a shower before walking them to the bus stops. Tanner comes running out the garage to inform me school is cancelled. Now, I have to tell you, I do not have good thoughts! I finish walking. Well, actually I was running because I was mad. This was not the plan for today. While I'm taking a shower, both girls are banging on the door the whole time. They think it would be so much fun if us girls all made cookies together. Well, yeehaw! Then Tanner greets me in the hallway with another weather report.

I go to the laundry room, and our washer machine is acting up again. It just stops washing and you have to bang the lid very hard a few times, and then it starts washing again. Well, I must have really banged it good because it started up again on the first bang. We go to the kitchen and make chocolate chip cookies, Troy's Grandma Patterson's recipe. They are flat and crunchy because that's how he likes cookies. I like them soft, but sometimes I have to say, "Happy man is my plan." I just made that up!

Back to the cookies. Tiana misses the whole bowl when she cracks the egg. Seriously, how can you miss a big bowl? I clean that up and get another weather report. Oh, did I mention the door frames are being smacked during all of this? We mix the cookies. The girls take turns singing the ABC song and then switch. Tanner comes around when it is time to clean out the bowl. That's my boy! I wash up the dishes while the cookies are baking. The girls are now wearing gymnastics outfits and doing flips on the couch. Troy calls to see how my day is going. I have no comment! Then I get another weather report.

Tanner decides to play against himself on the Wii. He likes to do that because then he is always a winner! Great, now the girls want to play the Wii too. There is a bowling tournament going on at the Pattersons! Well, that lasts ten minutes, just enough time for me to switch the laundry around and bang on the lid again. Tanner checks the computer for an up-to-date weather report. Did I mention the update is every fifteen minutes? That is four times an hour.

The girls decide to clean out Tessa's closet. Are you kidding me? That means disaster; I must interfere. The cookies are burning, according to Tanner. The phone rings. It is Troy, and he is just calling to see what I am doing. How sweet! I once again censor the words that want to come out of my mouth. Each kid talks to Daddy, which takes up ten minutes. Oops, time for another weather report. Tanner decides he should really let Grandma and Pop know about the weather. I say, "Go for it." Then all the kids take turns talking to Grandma. Pop is usually unavailable when we call!

Snack time—banana and apple. We have done the whole food allergy behavioral thing, hoping there was a connection with their mental illnesses. Nope, their mental illnesses have nothing to do with the food they eat. We just don't allow much sugar or caffeine. They all sit down and watch a show. It is amazing when this happens. I go on the computer to check my e-mail and Facebook.

Time for another weather report! The weather is really getting bad out! There is ice and snow. We have three to six inches coming. School will probably be cancelled tomorrow too. I'm just sayin'! I decide Tanner should call his special education teacher. She gave me her phone number; it's her fault! They have a nice chat. Then we get out beanie baby cards and decide to line the family room with the hundreds of cards. Well, isn't that a pretty carpet. I turn on music, and we sing while we lay out the cards.

Tanner is banging the door frames and pacing to each of the windows. There is a 100 percent chance of snow now. Watch out! Daddy calls—just when I had everything under control. He gets put on speaker phone and talks about how bad the roads are and how he was blocking the road for an accident. Thanks, Troy, that was a help. Bye, Daddy! Just make sure you can get home at 4:00.

At lunchtime, we eat Mexican pizza. Yum! I realize I never had breakfast. It's time for another weather report first. After lunch we play a matching game. We practice spelling words and read a story. Then we get another weather report. Grandma comes to visit! Yeah! She folds the big pile of laundry. I'm so glad she likes to do laundry. I'm just sayin'! Hey, let's lay all the beanie baby cards out again. Sure. But first Tanner has to give a weather update to Grandma.

I cut up an onion for supper; Tanner eats it as fast as I can chop. Tiana and I have been sending letters back and forth this afternoon. This is when she sometimes opens up. Tanner is our mailman. Tessa is writing a book. She is busy typing on the computer. Everything is calm as of right now. Tiana is being so good. I am just waiting; it is just too calm. We get another weather report from Tanner. Grandma says she must go home so she can tell Pop. Whatever!

We go out to shovel. The girls go looking for a friend to play with but come home with nobody. Tanner checks the weather report again. Daddy comes home. I take a fifteen-minute timeout for myself. I gave myself a come-to-Jesus meeting earlier. Now I am just thankful we made it through another day. We get another weather report. We have stuffed baked potatoes with chili on top for supper. Shower time. Tonight it is like a carwash, in and out fast. The kids waste a lot of water.

We sit down to have family devotions and pray. We watch the Christmas *Little House on the Prairie*. It's snowing. Why not! It's bedtime! But first one last weather report. Did I mention the weather reports come every fifteen minutes all day long? I'm just sayin'! I get Tiana and Tanner all tucked in. Tessa and I have a few minutes alone time to talk about the day, and then she is ready to sleep. Troy is on the treadmill during this time. All the kids are sleeping! Troy is taking a shower, and I am exhausted.

We watch IU (Indiana basketball), but they are having a pitiful year. I really wonder if the players can hear Troy yelling through the TV. I'm just sayin'! I can't see the players. I just see red running back and forth, which makes me tired, and I am ready for bed. Troy does his nightly routine. Then we kiss, say, "I love you," and put our masks on. Good night! God will never give me more than I can handle, but my prayer is, *Could there be school tomorrow, please!* Next thing I know Troy's work phone is ringing. It is 4:30 a.m., and they need him in early for the snow. Of course, the phone wakes up the whole house, because he has the ringer on high. So yep, my day begins at 4:30 a.m. too. Why do they have to be so chipper! Guess what? There is no delay; school is cancelled. I'm just sayin'! It's just another day in the life of the Patterson's.

It's an absolutely crazy life I am living, but "It Is Well with My Soul." I am ready to *see* God when my time on earth is done, but until then, I will not give up! No matter what.

Rival Soup

According to my Aunt Caro

Put half a stick of margarine in a pan on the stove, and turn it to low.

Peel and chunk many potatoes. I use eight-ish.

Put the potatoes in the melted butter, and then add water to cover the potatoes. Why in this order? 'Cause Aunt Caro says so!

Let them boil, and then mash the potatoes with a fork while they are still in the water.

Now the rivals, the best part!

Mix two cups of flour and two eggs together to make little dough crumbs/balls. Add the rivals to the water and boil for about thirteen minutes. Add half a package of Velveeta cheese cut into pieces. Add milk to the top of the pan and let the cheese melt. Season with salt and pepper.

It is absolutely heavenly! I'm just sayin'!

Acknowledgments

To my mom, thank you for always being there for us. You are only a phone call away, and that is so important. I am the person I am because of you!

To Pop, thank you for taking care of my mom all these years so I didn't have to worry about her. Bless your heart! I love both of you very much.

Brock, thank you for being a good big brother! You have a lot of the same characteristics as Dad. He would be so proud of all your accomplishments. I know I am.

Becky, thank you for sticking by our family through the good and the bad. You are the rock we can always lean on. If only we were like the Baxters, life would be perfect!

Brad, good luck in your future endeavors. We could really use a doctor in the family. No pressure! I'm just sayin'!

Ben, keep studying, because we definitely need our own computer guy. By the way, I am still hoping you will friend me on Facebook.

To the entire Patterson clan (and there are a lot of you), thank you for welcoming me into your family so many years ago. I am really glad I passed the initiation! Let's go make some more waves at the water park. Father Bob, I will see you at the golden gate! You know what I mean, *sniff.*

Aunt Caro, thank you for all your life lessons, cooking instructions, and medical advice over the years. You are so special to this family!

NAMI (National Alliance on Mental Illness), thank you for having an organization where we can speak our minds. Let's keep fighting for mental health, because we are family, no matter what!

Nick, thanks for being Tanner's best friend. I am so sorry your mom is gone, but we will all be with her again in heaven!

Morgan, thanks for being Tiana's monkey bar and locker partner. You are a true friend to our daughter!

To all of Tessa's friends, thanks for giving her a kind of normal childhood. She is lucky to have each of you in her life.

To the special teachers and staff at school, thank you for keeping our kids safe each day. Thank you for showing care to this hurting family. Bonnie S., you are the best counselor our family has ever had!

Wildcat Baseball League, thank you for giving our kids a chance to be accepted for who they are. The Patterson kids will be back each summer! Go Wildcats!

Pastor Dave and Jolene, thank you for loving us through all our faults and our faith-testing times. Thanks for really listening to us. I am ready to come drive the four-wheeler again. We'll bring the dessert and brats next time!

Special Olympics—let me win, but if I cannot win, let me be brave in the attempt.

To our friends & family, thank you for your many prayers & words of encouragement.

To my dad, thank you for giving me my life. You have been gone as long as you were a part of it and you are truly missed. I know you are watching from heaven. Can't wait to hear my daddy sing bass again!

To my Heavenly Father, thank you for teaching me how to climb all the mountains, big & small. You will never give me more than I can handle. Thank you for loving me, no matter what.

For more information, please contact the author at
www.climbingthemountains.net.